AKIYAH'S PRAYER BOOK

By Min. Byron Marshall

Copyright © 2018

ISBN: 978-1-987-77075-9

All rights reserved.

Printed in the United States of America.

Published & Illustrated by

THIS BOOK IS DEDICATED TO MY DAUGHTER AKIYAH

I LOVE YOU MORE THAN WORDS CAN EXPRESS.

Love,
Min. Byron Marshall
(Dad)

IT IS MY HOPE THAT THIS BOOK OF PRAYERS
MAY SERVE OUR GENERATION OF KIDS
AND FUTURE GENERATIONS TO COME.

I PRAY THAT THIS BOOK MAY INSPIRE
KIDS OF ALL AGES.

—Min. Byron Marshall

IN LOVING MEMORY OF

GRANNY BERNETTA J. WALKER
AUNT GLENDA "FAYE" BOSTON
AUNT BERNETTA K. WARD

Table of Contents

"A Thankful Prayer"

"A Birthday Prayer"

"A Prayer for Sharing"

"A Prayer for Good Sportsmanship"

"A Prayer for Obedience"

"A Prayer for Learning"

"A Prayer for Good Manners"

"A First Day of School Prayer"

"A Prayer for Loving Myself & Others"

"A Bedtime Prayer"

"A Thankful Prayer"

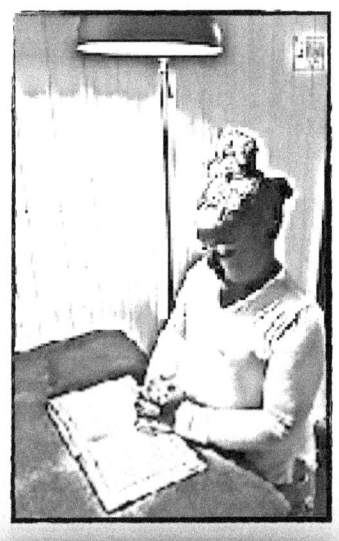

Thank you God for my life
and bless me Lord this day
to do the things that I so love
like laugh, and sing, and play.

Thank you God for my life
and bless us all this day
around the world, across the globe
make everything okay.

"A Birthday Prayer"

I am blessed to see this day
with everyone I love
to celebrate another year
I thank the Lord above.

For He alone has given me
the greatest gift I know
the very precious gift of life
for which I thank Him so.

"A Prayer for Sharing"

Teach us Lord to play together
and share our favorite toys
let us play with everyone
all the girls and boys.

We can draw, we can color
together you and I
sharing is so very fun
let's give it one good try.

"A Prayer for Good Sportsmanship"

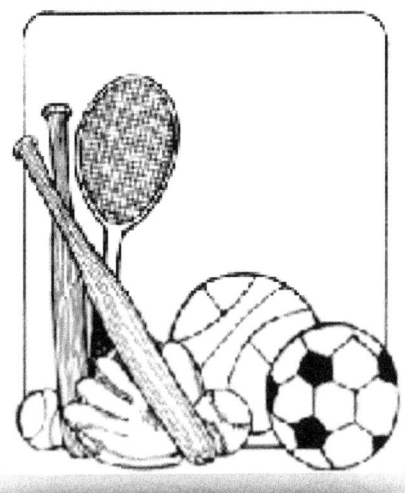

Lord we thank you for the chance
to play the sports we love
keep us safe from injury
and watch over us from above.

Let us never cheat to win
but play our games fair
let us always be good sports
and keep us in your care.

"A Prayer for Obedience"

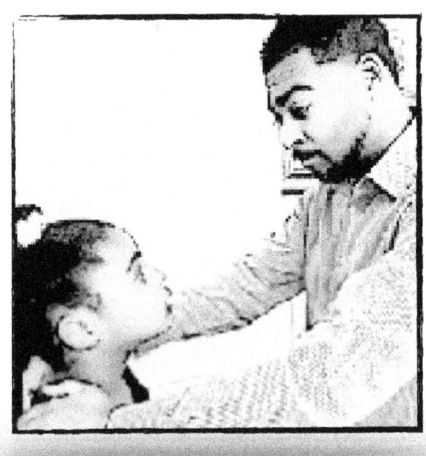

Lord I give to you my all
now with no delay
I listen closely to your voice
your will I shall obey.

I pray to honor my mother & father
so my days on earth are long
to follow all of your commands
in Christ to whom I belong.

"A Prayer for Learning"

Teach me Lord my alphabet
and how to read and write
teach me how to count to ten
and how to be polite.

Teach me all my shapes and colors
red, green, and blue
but most of all teach me Lord
to learn about you.

"A Prayer for Good Manners"

> THANK YOU
>
> I'M SORRY   PLEASE
>
> EXCUSE ME

Lord I pray for manners
to say and do what's right
I pray for good behavior
that's pleasing in thy sight.

I pray to say "excuse me"
"thank you" and "hello"
I pray to take good manners
everywhere I go.

"A First Day of School Prayer"

Bless me Lord today
on my first day of school
may I listen to my teachers
and follow all the rules.

Bless me to make studying
and learning my goal
to earn the good grades
and make the honor roll.

"A Prayer for Loving Myself & Others"

I am precious and unique
God made me his own way
He gave me special gifts and talents
to use for him each day.

I pray the love of God be spread
for all the world to see
to love each person as they are
just as God loves me.

"A Bedtime Prayer"

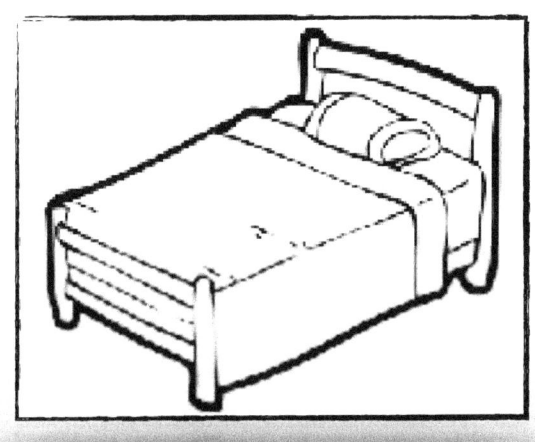

I thank you God for this day
at last the night is here
I pray you keep me safe and warm
your presence always near.

Protect this home and all within
please watch us from above
and may I sleep safe and sound
with comfort from your love.

COLORING ACTIVITY FOR KIDS

CPSIA information can be obtained
at www.ICGtesting.com
Printed in the USA
BVHW011151130919
558393BV00003B/47/P